The Frogs Want a King

Written by
Anita Loughrey

Illustrated by
Jenny Nightingale

In the deepest, largest pond in the land lived a family of frogs.

All the other creatures in the pond were eating their breakfast, but the frogs did not know what to eat.

"What should we eat today?" the big frog asked.

"I don't know," the medium-sized frog replied.

"I've no idea," the smallest frog croaked.

All the other creatures were playing in the pond, but the frogs did not know what to play.

"What should we play today?" the big frog asked.

"I have no idea," the medium-sized frog said.
"Nor have I," the smallest frog croaked.

All the other creatures were getting ready for bed, but the frogs did not know when to go to sleep.

"When should we go to sleep?" the big frog asked.

"I really have no idea," the medium-sized frog said.

"I don't know either," the smallest frog croaked.

"What we need is someone important to help us," the big frog said. "Then we would know what to do. They would tell us what to eat, what to play and when to go to sleep."

"What we need is a king," the smallest frog croaked.

"We should go to the great god Zeus and ask him to give us a king," the medium-sized frog said.

So the unhappy frogs hopped over the lily pads to see Zeus.

The biggest frog puffed out his neck and croaked loudly. "It is us, the frogs," he said. "We want you to give us a king."

"We need someone to tell us what to do," the smallest frog said.

After a few minutes, Zeus looked down at the frogs.

"I will give you a king," he said.

He waved his magic lightning staff and a log of wood appeared in the centre of the pond.

Zeus placed a gold crown at one end of the log. "Here is your king."

"Great wise king, what should we eat?" the big frog asked the log.

There was no reply. The log floated into the reeds, disturbing some flies. The flies buzzed into the air.

"Our great king said we should eat flies," the medium-sized frog said.

The frogs hopped up and down and happily ate the flies.

"Great, wise king what should we play?" the big frog asked the log.

There was no reply. The log bobbed up and down on the surface of the pond.

"Our great king said we should play 'bobbing up and down'," the smallest frog said.

The frogs played bobbing up and down.

"Great, wise king when should we go to sleep?" the smallest frog asked the log.

There was no reply. The log just floated quietly on the surface of the pond.

"Our great king is already asleep. We should go to sleep now," the biggest frog said.

So the frogs went straight to sleep.

One day the frogs decided to take a closer look at their king.

"Our king is so quiet. He never talks," the big frog said. "Perhaps he is ill."

The frogs hopped over to log and poked it. The gold crown fell into the water.

"It's just a log. We've been tricked," the smallest frog croaked.

So the unhappy frogs hopped back over the lily pads to see Zeus.

"Please give us a real king," the smallest frog croaked.

Zeus thought for a while. Then he said, "I will give you a new king. But be careful what you wish for."

Zeus waved his magic lightning staff and a crocodile appeared in the centre of the pond.

Zeus placed a gold crown on the crocodile's head.

"I am your new king," the crocodile said with a grin. The frogs saw two rows of sharp, white teeth.

"Great and powerful king, tell us what we should eat," the big frog said.

"You should eat frogs," the crocodile said.

"But **we** are frogs. We can't eat ourselves," the medium-sized frog said.

"But I can!" the crocodile said.

The crocodile snapped his sharp, white teeth.
The frogs dived quickly into the pond.

"Help us!" the smallest frog croaked.

Zeus waved his magic lightning staff and the crocodile vanished.

After that, the frogs agreed that they did not need a king to tell them what to do. They would decide what to eat, what to play and when to go to sleep on their own.

The moral of this fable is: don't complain about the way things are; the alternative may be far worse.